©1998 Northern Rockies Publishing
Rick and Susie Graetz
P.O. Box 1707, Helena, Montana 59624

Design by GingerBee Graphics

All color, design and prepress
work done in Montana, U.S.A.
Printed in Hong Kong
ISBN: 1-891152-017

Front Cover:

*Caprock at
Badland Breaks -
Makoshika State
Park near
Glendive.*

**SALVATORE
VASAPOLLI**

Preceeding page:

*The Piney Buttes
north of Jordan.*

**RICK AND SUSIE
GRAETZ**

This page:

*Sun River east of
Augusta.*

**RICK AND SUSIE
GRAETZ**

MONTANA
EAST OF THE MOUNTAINS

TEXT BY RICK GRAETZ
PHOTOGRAPHY BY RICK AND SUSIE GRAETZ
WITH CONTRIBUTIONS BY:

Peggy and Erwin Bauer ▪ Michael Crummett ▪ Chuck Haney
Michael Javorka ▪ Robert Lambing ▪ Dennis J. Lingohr ▪ Larry Mayer
Jim Mepham ▪ Salvatore Vasapolli ▪ Gus Wolfe ▪ George Wuerthner

INTRODUCTION

How do you portray a place that has so many pieces to it, with such distinct composition and moods? Representing Montana east of the mountains in words is not easy. Prose can't grasp the powerful aura and vastness of such an uncommon landscape. Nor can something on paper capture the feel of the wind, paint the colors of the enormous sky, characterize the seasons, or describe the sense of history that endures out here. And the camera can't take in all the eye can behold.

You have to see it. Only a firsthand experience will make you a believer. Let the words and photos of this book provoke and entice curiosity. Go see for yourself...go often and in every season.

Rick Graetz
Wolf Point, Montana
April 1, 1998

Sandstone spires of the Jerusalem Rocks near Sweetgrass.

CHUCK HANEY

Montana - East of the Mountains

Rick Graetz

A June evening a few years back found me at the site of Chief Joseph's surrender on the northern slopes of the Bear Paw Mountains. A thunderstorm was tailing off in a cloud laden sky. On the western horizon, a widening clear gap revealed a setting sun.

The elements and the heavens were joining in a prelude to an unfolding spectacle. Light hues of pink tinted the breaking clouds. The sun slowly dropped from sight. Pinks intensified and blended with shades of purple, blue, orange and red. A burning sky in all directions bathed the earth in enchanting light. To the east the Little Rockies glowed in gold, and on the south and north, distant lightning bolts accented the drama. Montana east of the mountains displayed itself in brilliant array.

Magnificent sunsets and sunrises are commonplace in this big land, a region that encompasses two-thirds of Montana. On the north, it stretches 460 miles from Browning and the east slopes of Glacier National Park to the North Dakota line just beyond Sidney. Its central boundary begins in the valley of the upper Musselshell River, near Harlowton, and reaches for 300 miles to our state's eastern edge. In the south, from Red Lodge and the east face of the Beartooth Mountains, it's 250 miles as the eagle flies along the Wyoming border to the South Dakota line. On its western flank, the sweep of the terrain is halted abruptly by the imposing Rocky Mountain Front. Turning east, it flows gently into the Dakotas. In-between the landforms of this corner of the Great Plains are a wonderful diverse mix of high prairie, island mountain ranges, buttes, badlands, river canyons, wilderness grasslands, wildlife refuges, lakes and rolling hills.

At first it seems overpowering…the openness, the immensity and the distances. Gradually, though, you get comfortable with it all. Then you notice the beauty and splendor. Not just imposing geologic structures, but also an abundance of simple grandeur…cottonwoods along a small creek; a lone tree silhouetted on a hillside; waves of wheat dancing in the summer wind; the first rays of sun illuminating sandstone cliffs; delicate snow patterns drifted

"Charlie Russell" Square Butte, south-west of Great Falls.
RICK AND SUSIE GRAETZ

Facing page:
Wind power south of Malta.
RICK AND SUSIE GRAETZ

*Young Creek
on the Bar V
Ranch in
the Wolf
Mountains.*
**RICK AND
SUSIE GRAETZ**

*Facing page:
Antelope freely
roam the
prairies.*
**ERWIN AND
PEGGY BAUER**

against a weathered barn; the northern lights shimmering across the night sky; antelope moving quietly through sagebrush-covered prairie and the soft fusion of earth and sky on horizons that seem endless. There are also striking features...the thousand foot deep canyons of the Missouri River; the enormity of Fort Peck Lake; stately prairie buttes; isolated mountains including the Little Rockies, Big Snowies, Bear Paw, Judith and Sweetgrass Hills; the Makoshika and Terry badlands and the canyons of the Bighorn.

Montana's mightiest waterways have carved their routes through this territory. Born of mountain snows and springs, the prairie gives them room to grow. They are fabled waters...the Missouri, the Yellowstone, the Marias, the Judith, the Bighorn, the Powder, the Tongue, the Milk and the Musselshell. The wide Missouri and the free-flowing Yellowstone served as routes of exploration for Meriwether Lewis, William Clark and other adventurers. The Missouri witnessed steamboat travel to Fort Benton... Montana's birthplace.

In legend, scenic beauty and recreation, the Missouri stands out. It passes silently through some of the most remote and least inhabited country in the West. Nearly 150 miles of the river have been designated as Wild and Scenic...protected forever. Its eastern reaches meander through the rugged Missouri Breaks and the huge Charles M. Russell Wildlife Refuge. At Fort Peck, a dam has turned the river into the fourth-largest reservoir in the world—175-mile long Fort Peck Lake, a Montana treasure with a shoreline of 1,600 miles.

The Missouri's flow is launched at the meeting of the waters near Three Forks in western Montana. Here the Madison, Jefferson and Gallatin Rivers join to power the big Missouri. En route east, it picks up more volume from the Dearborn, Teton, Marias, Judith, Musselshell, Milk and other rivers.

The Yellowstone, no small stream, provides recreation, irrigation and beauty to eastern Montana. Explorers named it La Roche Jaune, French for "yellow stone." This, the largest undammed river left in North America, begins its flow from Younts Peak south of Yellowstone National Park in the Wyoming high country. From there it rushes 670 miles to meet the Missouri in North Dakota, just beyond the Montana line. It gathers strength in its lower reaches from the Little Bighorn, Tongue and Powder River flows.

With the exception of some stretches of the Yellowstone, most of the rivers of the high plains are mellow—no whitewater excitement, just serenity, solitude, beauty and a sense of the past. The water moves at an easy pace past islands, sandbars and groves of cottonwoods interspersed with a carpet of grass; home to river wildlife. And the landscape along the rivers has changed little with time. A floater can imagine nineteenth-century fur trappers and explorers sharing the same space.

These eastern Montana lands are Big Sky Country. Subdued topography allows the sky main billing. It is the canvas for beautiful displays of the sun, morning and evening, and billowing clouds. With nightfall, this sky presents an astronomer's dream of brilliant nocturnal displays... stars over the Judith Basin on a cold winter night, a full moon illuminating the hills between Scobey and Plentywood and meteors streaking off in any direction. It is as big a dome of sky as any on the planet and brings, on some days, an early morning and evening light so beautiful that no painter or photographer could ever duplicate it.

And with the sky comes the wind. Out here the breeze has range on it and character. As it rakes the land, it gives clarity and cleanliness to everything—there's no haze diluting the panorama. The wind can bring ferocious blizzards, snow-eating chinooks and the pleasant smell of sweet clover. It can sustain a tempered clip one day and a hurricane force the next. A day without it seems boring.

While the wind adds personality to eastern Montana's prairie, the seasons give it color. Each time of the year is distinct, but spring shows off the land at its best. A morning in early May dawns raw and gray...intermittent snowflakes make an effort to prolong a fading plains winter. But this day the promise of the equinox is about to be fulfilled. The warmth of a rising sun endures. The prairie has turned to face spring.

At first the sagebrush and grasses convert to a vibrant green. Wheat fields come to life and the juniper and scattered pines show signs of new growth. Later in the month a rainbow of wildflowers joins the celebration. In June this new beginning moves up the mountainsides and buttes. Spring moisture and the thunderstorms of early summer keep the landscape fresh.

As July heads towards August and rainfall lessens, vegetation cures and gold and brown prevail. The grasses take on a warm dust color. This is the hot, dry period. In September and early October, the summer yellows become mixed with autumn's flame-orange cottonwoods in the river bottoms and the reds of low-lying vegetation in the coulees and on the hillsides. The sky can be cloudless for days.

Sometime in November, winds from the north signal the start of winter. By now fall snowstorms have put a coating of white on the upper reaches of the Big Snowies and most of the other mountains. Lasting snows begin spreading to some areas of the prairie and the Missouri Breaks. Soon cold, strong winds will deposit snowdrifts of every size and shape imaginable. Hillsides will be swept clean and ice will form on the rivers. Winter's harshness also brings a softness...tall golden grass and dark evergreens contrast against a blanket of white... and delicate sunsets and sunrises replace summer's blazing displays. The landscape is at rest. This is the prairie's quiet time.

In the western reaches of the prairie country, winter brings a phenomenon known as a chinook...the snow eater. These mild winds bring tempo-

*Black Butte
and the Judith
Mountains near
Lewistown.*
LARRY MAYER

rary respite from the frigid atmosphere that descends on Montana. Chinooks come to life as warm, water-laden air soars up over the Great Divide and drops its moisture. The wind heats up as it rushes downslope heading east. This force pushes the cold air in residence over the plains into oblivion and causes dramatic temperature rises, up to 30 and 40 degrees in an hour.

A chinook's presence is also visible in the sky in the form of a "chinook" arch of clouds, at once dark and beautiful. If the sun catches it just right, a stunning sunset paints the arch, embellishing the entire sky with a multitude of colors. A chinook can end as quickly as it arrives, with the push of a ferocious northern blizzard reclaiming its season.

Mountains make western Montana, but east of the Rockies they are only a modest share of a diverse province, appearing as islands floating in a big sea. None are lofty, but where they rise from the prairie they make their presence known. The views from their summits are far-reaching and impressive. They are the Little Rockies, the Sweetgrass Hills, the Bear Paw, the Highwoods, the Little Belts, the Moccasins, the Judith, the Big and Little Snowies, the Bull, Pryor, Bighorn, Rosebud, Sheep and Wolf Mountains. These highlands serve as watersheds, wildlife sanctuaries and respites from summer heat. They harbor forests of Ponderosa pine, Douglas-fir, aspen and willows. Ecologically, some are mini-versions of the mountains of the Continental Divide. Others are a blend of prairie and alpine zones.

The Big Snowies, in the center of Montana, provide a high stage to view a dozen mountain ranges. From the summit of 8,681-foot Great House Peak, a hiker can gaze at a 300-mile-long view, northwest to the Sweetgrass Hills and south to the Beartooth Mountains.

As Lewis and Clark made their way westward, the first rise of rocks they viewed were the Little Rocky Mountains. The natives called them the Wolf Mountains. White people came to them for their gold and they hid outlaws.

One of Montana's most prominent ski areas, Showdown, is centered in the Little Belts, the largest of Montana's outlying ranges.

Ice caves, wild horses and a desert environment below their southern slopes make the Pryors an attraction. With the Bighorn Mountains, they guard the narrowed canyons holding 67-mile-long Bighorn Lake and Bighorn National Recreation Area.

Other elevated features mark the Montana prairies. The Medicine Rocks and Chalk Buttes stand as silent sentinels in southeastern Montana's cowboy country. Black Butte, on the eastern rise of the Judith Mountains, can be seen from more than 50 miles away. Charlie Russell used the imposing Square Butte near Geraldine and the larger Square Butte, southwest of Great Falls, as backgrounds for his famous paintings.

Badlands and river breaks add to the fascination of Montana east of the Rockies. Shaped by wind and water, places such as Makoshika, the Terry Badlands, the Piney Buttes and the Missouri and Yellowstone breaks present vivid colors, a wild landscape and a country void of people.

And, of course, there are the grasslands. In some areas they are flat, in most gently undulating, dissected by coulees and marked in places with sandstone formations…parts of a serene environment accentuated by space and the sound of the wind.

Before the arrival of white travelers, the land stretching east of Montana's Northern Rockies was a wildlife kingdom and a vast native hunting ground. Millions of bison, great herds of antelope, timber wolves and grizzly bears were common. The wild bison are now gone and the grizzlies have retreated to the mountains, but the prairie is still home to an enormous population of big animals, small critters and winged creatures. Turkeys, burrowing owls, white pelicans, elk, ospreys, deer, blue herons, pronghorn antelope, Canada geese, sandhill cranes, cormorants, ducks, foxes, eagles, bighorn sheep, pheasants, coyotes, Hungarian partridge, grouse, prairie dogs and more than 200 species of birds are some of the wild residents of Great Plains Montana.

Montana's eastern regions present wildlife displays unlike anywhere else. The spectacle of flights of ducks and geese landing to gather on prairie waters in the fall before migrating south…the excitement of spring as they head home again to refuges, lakes and wetlands scattered from the east slope to the Dakotas…the peculiar spring mating dance of the sharptail grouse. Plenty of space, minimal human activity and protected lands ensure thriving wildlife.

Together, Medicine Lake National Wildlife Refuge, tucked up in Montana's northeast corner and Bowdoin National Wildlife Refuge out of Malta make a home for more than 200,000 ducks and geese, as well as lake pelicans. Other havens, such as Half-Breed National Wildlife Refuge at Rapelje, Freezeout Lake near Choteau and War Horse Lake National Wildlife Refuge northwest of Winnett, also attract migratory congregations.

Then there is one of America's special places… the wild, remote and beautiful Charles M. Russell Wildlife Refuge…1,100,000 acres in a 200-mile strip encircling Fort Peck Lake. Its deep canyons, rough river breaks and isolation provide a sanctuary for wildlife, big and small. It includes the UL Bend Wilderness, home ground for native elk and transplanted bighorn sheep.

Not enough can be said about fishing in these parts beyond the mountains. The catching of warm water game fish in all the area's lakes and rivers inspires stories. Fort Peck Lake and segments of the Missouri River are the most legendary of all. Walleye, northern pike, lake trout and chinook salmon are just a few of the breeds found in these waters.

The walleye rate their own tournaments, attracting some of the nation's best fishing enthusiasts as entrants. Parts of Fort Peck Lake and the Milk, Missouri and Yellowstone Rivers furnish the necessary habitat for the almost

A mallard duck is cleared for take-off.

ERWIN AND PEGGY BAUER

Facing page: Medicine Lake National Wildlife Refuge, 31,000 acres of lake, wetlands and prairie offers protection to numerous birds, animals and plants.

RICK AND SUSIE GRAETZ

At 245,000 acres Fort Peck Lake is the world's second largest earth-fill reservoir.

LARRY MAYER

prehistoric paddlefish, which average 80 pounds. The largest ever taken was a 142-pound giant caught in the Missouri, upstream from Fort Peck Lake.

Rainbow and brown trout live in the upper reaches of the Marias, Judith, Milk, Teton and Musselshell Rivers. The Bighorn River, fed by the cold waters of Bighorn Lake, is considered one of the best rainbow and brown trout fisheries on earth.

History out here spans a short and wild time. It is recent and evident. Only 125 years ago Indian nations hunted the enormous bison herds that thundered across Montana territory. They had the plains to themselves, wandering freely in search of food and shelter. Then the 1804-1806 Lewis and Clark expedition changed the face of the land and the native culture forever. This Corps of Discovery marked the way for the white invaders. At first, the newcomers came in search of beaver pelts and routes west—mountain men, trappers, traders and explorers. Soon steamboats began plying the Missouri to Fort Benton. The first one reached Fort McKenzie, just below Fort Benton, in 1859. Gold seekers followed, combing the gulches of the Judith Mountains and Little Rockies. More people entered Indian lands.

Grass was rich, thick and free for the taking. Central and eastern Montana had what seemed an endless supply. By the 1870s, western Montana stockmen ventured into the lush river bottoms and tall grass to the east, laying claim to the vast open range. They were joined by the legendary "long drives" of Longhorns, up 1800 miles from Texas to winter in Montana.

The era of the big ranches had begun. The Circle C and DHS ranches located in the country between Malta and Lewistown became Montana symbols. These times bred rustlers, horse thieves, cattle barons and vigilantes. The myths and reality of the American cowboy took root. Outlaws met with frontier justice handed out by "Stuart's Stranglers," named for prominent rancher Granville Stuart. The natives took their last stand during this time and lost. The bison were gone and the white man was too powerful. A culture and way of life all but disappeared from eastern Montana.

The cattlemen were to have their freedom curtailed as well. The tough winter of 1886-87 caused heavy livestock losses and began the decline of the large operations. An estimated 360,000 head of cattle perished in that particularly cruel winter. Blizzards swept in from Canada bringing continuous snow. A December thaw lasted only long enough to melt the upper layers, then a freeze sealed off the ground. In January more snow and temperatures 50 to 60 degrees below zero arrived. It was March before it ended. A horse wrangler working for a Judith Basin outfit sketched an image of a starving cow on the cover of a shoebox to describe the situation to his bosses…"The Last of the 5,000" or "Waiting for a Chinook." Charlie Russell had started his rise to fame painting a vanishing west.

During the 1880s, railroads were pushing their way into Montana from the Dakotas. The Great Northern, Milwaukee Road and Northern Pacific lines brought farmers to plow the virgin sod and fence the land. The cattle empires, weakened by winter, shrunk further as the open grasslands diminished. Sheep moved in on the cattle and by 1900, outnumbered cows on the prairie. For a while, Montana was the number one wool-producing state in the nation.

At the turn of the century, railroad promotions and the building of towns along the steel roads coupled with generous homestead laws to bring a wave of people to eastern Montana. They arrived from points east in the USA and from Europe to cultivate riches from the soil. Some prospered, but many didn't. The time of the homesteader peaked in 1918. Wet years evaporated...drought and low prices set in. Thousands left their places never to return. Prairie vegetation gradually reclaimed fields that once produced bountiful harvests.

Remnants and vivid reminders of early day eastern Montana are everywhere. Parts of former travel byways such as the Great North Trail, the Nez Perce Trail, the Wood Mountain Trail, the Whoop-Up Trail and the Pony Express Route are still visible as are the ruins of forts, trading posts and stagecoach stops. Undisturbed areas show signs of travois tracks, wagon wheel ruts and teepee rings. Old buildings that once housed settlers and their dreams still stand. They now serve as refuges for birds and owls and are often surrounded by tall grass or plowed fields.

Although the drought ended the hopes of many, some persisted and stayed on. These folks and their sons and daughters, are part of the backbone of the Montana prairie country of today. They don't crowd the landscape, but rather live on farms and ranches well apart from their neighbors or in small towns with colorful names...Sunburst, Judith Gap, Roundup, Cut Bank, Plentywood, Whitewater, Choteau, Big Sandy, Chinook, Lame Deer, Lodge Grass, Ekalaka, Grassrange and Wolf Point as well as Billings, Great Falls, Lewistown and Miles City. The latter four, large towns by Montana standards, are just small places on the vast Montana plains.

The distance between communities is comfortable; elbowroom is plentiful and space dwarfs the human presence. High school basketball teams often travel for games up to 300 miles—one-way. The population is dispersed enough to support one-teacher schools. About 67 of them are still open east of the Rockies. Most consist of grades one through eight with an average of fifteen students.

Many of the citizens' roots are in agriculture, by far the mainstay of the economy and the activity that gives Montana's northern plains their sturdy character. Livestock operations and dry land farming are the major pursuits, and most of the cultivation involves wheat.

18

Abandoned ranch buildings south of Moore. The Big Snowy Mountains in the distance.

RICK AND SUSIE GRAETZ

Facing page:
A grain elevator stands guard near Dutton.

JOHN LAMBING

Winter wheat is planted in late summer and gains a foothold before the cold descends. It renews growth with spring's warmth and is harvested in July. Montana's dominant crop, it crowds the horizon of The Golden Triangle...the country north and northwest of Great Falls. Farther east and north, where winter is colder, spring wheat colors the fields. Seeds are sown at winter's end and the crop is cut in late summer. Yields tend to be lower with this strain of wheat.

Beyond the mountains, strip farming is a hallmark. In heavily cultivated areas, successions of wheat, interspersed with fallow earth, stretch as far as the eye can see. This farming practice serves as a deterrent to wind erosion and conserves moisture. Each year the pattern is reversed.

Sugar beet farming doesn't create the same scenic mosaic as the ribbons of wheat fields do, but in the valley of the Yellowstone River, especially between Laurel and Glendive, it adds to the well-being of southeast Montana.

While the big unfenced places of the mid- to late 1800s are gone, cattle are still very important on Montana's high plains. Cowboys continue to work the range and substantial ranches exist in Yellowstone and surrounding counties. Miles City in Custer County is known as the "Cattle Capital of Montana."

Montana's Indians also survived the devastation of their homelands and are a prominent part of this piece of the Big Sky Country. They are the Blackfeet, the Chippewa, the Cree, the Crow, the Northern Cheyenne, the Assiniboine, the Gros Ventre and the Sioux nations. Some still occupy a portion of their ancestral grounds; others do not. Most live on six reservations scattered throughout the Northern Plains. Powwows, rodeos, Milk River Indian Days, North American Indian Days and the Crow Fair are tributes to their proud tribal traditions.

As the first residents of Montana, these natives were good stewards of the land. They respected it and took only what they needed to survive. They passed through and left it as they found it. Their legacy is still present out here in the places that have remained unaltered with the passing of the ages, and their spirit is still carried on the wind. Listen for it and feel it as you explore and marvel at Montana east of the mountains.

Sandstone formations. The Big Sheep Mountains in the distance - near Circle.

RICK AND SUSIE GRAETZ

Top:
Harvested wheat patterns near Cut Bank.
JOHN LAMBING

Bottom:
Dancer at the Crow Fair.
MICHAEL CRUMMETT

Following page:
Square Butte near Geraldine.
SALVATORE VASAPOLLI

Facing page:

Missouri River south of Culbertson.

RICK AND SUSIE GRAETZ

Top:

Beauty is found on a back road west of Lewistown.

RICK AND SUSIE GRAETZ

Bottom:

The Fergus County courthouse in Lewistown. A spot on main street is the exact location of the center of Montana.

RICK AND SUSIE GRAETZ

*Chester is a
wheat farming
community
situated on the
Hi-Line.*
**RICK AND SUSIE
GRAETZ**

*Facing page:
Thunderstorms
bring wildflowers
to life.*
**MICHAEL
JAVORKA**

*Following page:
Sunset on the
Missouri River
between
Bainville and
Fairview.*
**RICK AND SUSIE
GRAETZ**

Facing page:
The Powder River
near Mizpah,
southeast of
Miles City.
RICK AND SUSIE
GRAETZ

Top:
Fall colors in the
Spring Creek
bottoms between
Ekalaka and
Powderville.
RICK AND SUSIE
GRAETZ

Bottom:
Northern
Saw-Whet owl.
ERWIN AND
PEGGY BAUER

Following page:
Sun Dance lodges -
Rocky Boys
Reservation - home
of the Chippewa
and Cree people -
south of Havre.
MICHAEL
CRUMMETT

Top:
Bighorn
Canyon.
RICK AND SUSIE
GRAETZ

34

Bottom:
Sandstone
outcroppings
carved by the
wind were
considered
sacred by
the Indians.
Medicine Rocks
State Park near
Ekalaka.
RICK AND SUSIE
GRAETZ

Facing page:
Prairie country
looking north
from outside
Roy. The
Little Rocky
Mountains in
the distance.
RICK AND SUSIE
GRAETZ

Facing page:
The Wild and
Scenic Missouri
River near
Eagle Creek.
WAYNE
MUMFORD

Missouri River
near Oswego.
RICK AND SUSIE
GRAETZ

Following page:
The Chalk Buttes
easily seen for
miles have long
served as land-
marks for those
traveling through
the southeastern
corner of the state.
RICK AND SUSIE
GRAETZ

Top:

From the Ulm Pishkun Buffalo Jump looking towards the town of Ulm.

RICK AND SUSIE GRAETZ

Bottom:

Weaning calves at the Bar V Ranch in the Wolf Mountains near Decker.

RICK AND SUSIE GRAETZ

Facing page:

Evening light brightens one of the grain elevators at Madoc between Scobey and Plentywood.

RICK AND SUSIE GRAETZ

43

Facing page:
A badland's ranch
between Bainville
and Snowden.
RICK AND SUSIE
GRAETZ

Top:
The Poplar River
Valley on the Fort
Peck Indian
Reservation south
of Scobey.

Bottom:
Prairie east of Malta.
RICK AND SUSIE
GRAETZ

Following page:
The Tongue River
in late summer.
JOHN LAMBING

Top:

A solitary church stands alone on the prairie north of Poplar.
RICK AND SUSIE GRAETZ

Bottom:

Sage grouse perform a unique mating ritual, returning each year to the same grounds. Charles M. Russell National Wildlife Refuge.
DENNIS LINGOHR

Facing page:
Big Sheep Mountains and strip farming west of Sidney.
RICK AND SUSIE GRAETZ

Following page:
Bighorn River.
WAYNE MUMFORD

Facing page:
Toadstool
sandstone
formation. The
Badlands north
of Jordan.
RICK AND SUSIE
GRAETZ

5 1

Top:
Sunrise off of the
Haxby road,
northeast of
Jordan.
RICK AND SUSIE
GRAETZ

Bottom:
The Little
Bighorn Battle-
field National
Monument near
Crow Agency.
MICHAEL
CRUMMETT

Following page:
Where the prairie
meets the moun-
tains. The Rocky
Mountain Front.
RICK AND SUSIE
GRAETZ

*Prairie north
of Scobey.*
**RICK AND SUSIE
GRAETZ**

Facing page:
*Crystal Lake in
the Big Snowy
Mountains.*
**GEORGE
WUERTHNER**

Following page:
The Terry Badlands.
CHUCK HANEY

Facing page:
The Yellowstone River near Columbus.
RICK AND SUSIE GRAETZ

Top:
The Missouri River Breaks near Winifred.
CHUCK HANEY

Bottom:
Agriculture is the leading economic activity in eastern Montana. West of Circle.
RICK AND SUSIE GRAETZ

Top:

Migrating birds use Freezeout Lake, southeast of Choteau, as a refuge and resting spot.

RICK AND SUSIE GRAETZ

Bottom:

The Little Rockies from the southeast.

RICK AND SUSIE GRAETZ

Facing page:

In the South Hills of Billings looking towards the Pryor Mountains.

RICK AND SUSIE GRAETZ

Following page:

A fall freeze quiets the landscape north of Billings.

RICK AND SUSIE GRAETZ

Facing page:
West of Winnett.
RICK AND SUSIE GRAETZ

65

Top:
A famous landmark, Pompeys Pillar, was named by William Clark in 1806 when he and the Corps of Discovery sighted it on their journey down the Yellowstone River.
LARRY MAYER

Bottom:
Billings - The state's largest town is physically defined by the Rimrocks that surround it.
RICK AND SUSIE GRAETZ

A summer storm clears over the Little Rockies.
RICK AND SUSIE GRAETZ

Facing page:
Off of the "Lost Highway," out of Sidney.
RICK AND SUSIE GRAETZ

Following page:
South of Sidney in the Yellowstone River Breaks.
RICK AND SUSIE GRAETZ

Facing page:

Bighorn Canyon from the sacred Indian vision site Pretty Eagle.

RICK AND SUSIE GRAETZ

Top:

Little Dry Creek east of Jordan.

RICK AND SUSIE GRAETZ

Bottom:

Osprey.

GUS WOLFE

Top:

Late spring in the Bear Paw Mountains or Bears Paw or Bear Paws. There is a controversy as to which is correct. The most widely accepted name is the Bear Paw Mountains.

RICK AND SUSIE GRAETZ

Bottom:

At an elevation of 3,084 feet Blue Mountain north of Wibaux is the highest point in extreme north-eastern Montana.

RICK AND SUSIE GRAETZ

Facing page:

The Musselshell River near Ryegate in central Montana.

RICK AND SUSIE GRAETZ

Following page:

East of Powderville.

RICK AND SUSIE GRAETZ

Facing page:
A prairie sunset west of Great Falls.
RICK AND SUSIE GRAETZ

Top:
Rich with history from Lewis and Clark to western artist Charlie Russell, Great Falls is also called The Electric City.
RICK AND SUSIE GRAETZ

Bottom:
Fireweed blossoms and a white-tailed fawn.
ERWIN AND PEGGY BAUER

78

Top:

Cottonwood Creek north of Malta from the road to Loring.

RICK AND SUSIE GRAETZ

Bottom:

Muddy Creek north of Redstone.

RICK AND SUSIE GRAETZ

Facing page:

Crown Butte and the town of Simms.

RICK AND SUSIE GRAETZ

Following page:

The "Moon Garden" north of Jordan.

RICK AND SUSIE GRAETZ

Facing page:
The Powder
River as the old
saying goes is "a
mile wide and
an inch deep."
RICK AND SUSIE
GRAETZ

Top:
The east face of
the Beartooth
Mountains
north of Red
Lodge.
RICK AND SUSIE
GRAETZ

Bottom:
Agriculture
plays an impor-
tant role in the
economy of
Sidney.
RICK AND SUSIE
GRAETZ

*The Four Buttes
west of Scobey
were at one time
called Whiskey
Buttes due to the
practice of
trading liquor
with the Indians.*
**RICK AND SUSIE
GRAETZ**

Facing page:
*Pryor
Mountains.*
**WAYNE
MUMFORD**

Following page:
Powder River.
**RICK AND SUSIE
GRAETZ**

Top:

Whitetail is located on Whitetail Creek only seven miles from the Canadian border in northeastern Montana.

RICK AND SUSIE GRAETZ

Bottom:

Larkspur and lupine.

JIM MEPHAM

Facing page:

Lewis and Clark's decision point. The confluence of the Marias and Missouri rivers.

RICK AND SUSIE GRAETZ

Facing page:
The Missouri River near Fort Benton.
RICK AND SUSIE GRAETZ

Top:
The Yellowstone River south of Sidney.
RICK AND SUSIE GRAETZ

Bottom:
Bowdoin National Wildlife Refuge.
RICK AND SUSIE GRAETZ

Top:

Looking east from the Little Rockies.

RICK AND SUSIE GRAETZ

Bottom:

Mountain sheep are found in the UL Bend Wilderness and UL Bend National Wildlife Refuge south of Malta.

ERWIN AND PEGGY BAUER

Facing page:

Fort Peck Lake near Hell Creek.

RICK AND SUSIE GRAETZ

Following page:

Capitol Rock is a nationally registered landmark northeast of Alzada.

SALVATORE VASAPOLLI

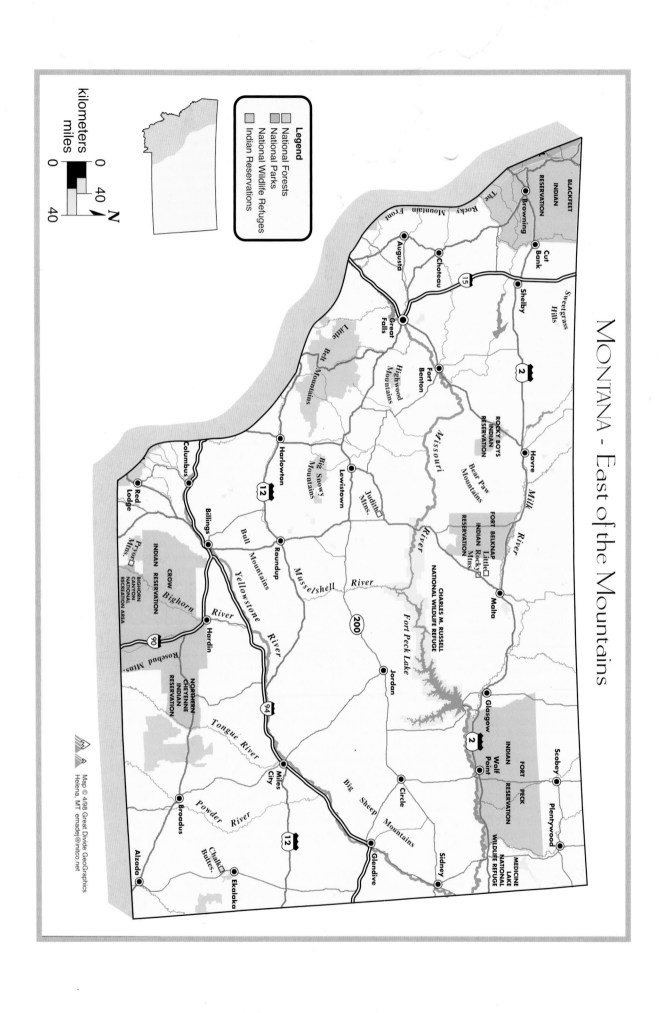

MONTANA - East of the Mountains

Legend
National Forests
National Parks
National Wildlife Refuges
Indian Reservations

N

kilometers
0   40
miles
0   40

Map © 4/98 Great Divide GeoGraphics
Helena, MT emadej@mlico.net

BLACKFEET INDIAN RESERVATION
Browning
Cut Bank
Augusta
Choteau
Shelby
Sweetgrass Hills
The Rocky Mountain Front
Great Falls
Little Belt Mountains
Highwood Mountains
Fort Benton
Missouri River
ROCKY BOYS INDIAN RESERVATION
Bear Paw Mountains
Havre
Milk River
FORT BELKNAP INDIAN RESERVATION
Little Rocky Mtns.
Harlowton
Big Snowy Mountains
Lewistown
Judith Mtns.
CHARLES M. RUSSELL NATIONAL WILDLIFE REFUGE
Malta
Columbus
Red Lodge
Billings
Bull Mountains
Roundup
Musselshell River
Fort Peck Lake
Jordan
Glasgow
Wolf Point
FORT PECK INDIAN RESERVATION
Scobey
Plentywood
Pryor Mtns.
BIGHORN CANYON NATIONAL RECREATION AREA
CROW INDIAN RESERVATION
Bighorn River
Yellowstone River
Hardin
Rosebud Mtns.
NORTHERN CHEYENNE INDIAN RESERVATION
Tongue River
Miles City
Big Sheep Mountains
Circle
Sidney
MEDICINE LAKE NATIONAL WILDLIFE REFUGE
Broadus
Powder River
Chalk Buttes
Alzada
Ekalaka
Glendive

15
2
12
200
94
90
2
12